Dressed to Impress: 1840–1914

Christina Walkley

B.T. Batsford Ltd, London

© Christina Walkley 1989
First published 1989

All rights reserved. No part of this publication
may be reproduced, in any form or by any means,
without permission from the Publisher

ISBN 0 7134 60105

Typeset by Speedlith Photo Litho Limited
Longford Trading Estate, Thomas Street, Manchester M32 0JT
and printed in Great Britain by
The Bath Press, Bath
for the publishers
B. T. Batsford Ltd
4 Fitzhardinge Street
London W1H 0AH

back jacket photo:
*Mary Abigail Williams in her wedding dress, 1865. The dress is
pale mauve corded watered silk, trimmed with cream lace and mauve
silk ribbon, frayed to imitate swansdown. (Gallery of English
Costume, Platt Hall, Manchester)*

end papers:
A picnic in Lindley Wood, c. 1895. (Publisher's Collection)

Sources of Illustrations

The photographs in this book are reproduced by courtesy of the following: figs 2, 14, 27, 29, 58, 66, 67, 68, 69, 70, 79, 83, 87, 88, 90, 105–the Museum of Costume and Fashion Research Centre, Bath; figs 4, 8, 10, 11, 15, 18, 20, 28, 53, 85, 94–the BBC Hulton Picture Library; fig. 55–Birmingham Museum and Art Gallery; figs 39, 40, 41, 42–Cadbury Limited; figs 13, 21, 45, 46, 47, 48, 49–Colman's of Norwich; figs 12, 19, 30, 36, 37, 38, 52, 74, 75, 76, 104, 107, 108–the Dorset Natural History and Archaeological Society, Dorset County Museum, Dorchester; figs 86, 91, 92, 93–the Gallery of English Costume, Platt Hall, Manchester; 17, the Local History Library, Manchester; fig. 98–the North Devon Athenaeum; fig. 82–the proprietors of Punch; fig. 33–the Institute of Agricultural History and Museum of English Rural Life, University of Reading; fig. 32–the Berkshire Archaeological Society and Reading Museum; figs 43, 44, Rowntree plc; figs 34, 106–the Royal Institution of Cornwall; fig. 9–the Trustees of the Tate Gallery; figs 35, 51, 84, 102, 110–Yeovil Museum. Figs 1, 3, 6, 22, 23, 24, 25, 61, 62, 71, 72, 73, 78, 80, 81 and 89 are from private owners; the remaining photographs are from the Publisher's collection.

For Carolyn : For Angela

Acknowledgements

I am deeply grateful to the staff of all the museums and archives mentioned in the list of sources for their help in selecting interesting material, especially Penny Byrde at the Fashion Research Centre, Bath; Judy Morris at the Dorset County Museum; Anthea Jarvis at the Gallery of English Costume, Manchester; and Moira Gittos at Yeovil Museum. I am also greatly indebted to the individuals who gave me access to their family albums: Hilary Barlow-Poole, Major and Mrs Hall, Elizabeth Hawkins, Frances Moule, John Newton, Viv Probert and Bonny Sartin. I should like to acknowledge additional help from Jane Badger, John and Lin Lifford, Gerald Pitman and Julian Treuherz. Finally, I want to thank my husband Phill for his consistent enthusiasm and valuable advice; and Angela Hamm, Veronica Hansford and Christine Legrand who made this book possible by looking after my son Toby.

Introduction

Everybody likes dressing up for a special occasion, and throughout history the rich and leisured have enjoyed creating excuses for wearing expensive and beautiful clothes. The Victorians and Edwardians were no exception to this rule, and in terms of quantity of material, elaboration of trimming, and expenditure of human effort, they could hold their own against anybody.

High Society

The social life of the aristocracy throughout this era naturally revolved around the royal family, and thus the ultimate social accolade was to be presented at court. During the nineteenth century the upper classes found themselves having to accommodate growing numbers of people whose wealth and success owed nothing to birth and everything to business acumen and sheer hard work; they reacted by making their admission procedures increasingly formal and ritualized. Presentation at court was by no means restricted to debutantes: anyone might qualify who had recently enjoyed professional or social advancement of some kind, perhaps by contracting a brilliant marriage, or who had otherwise earned the sovereign's notice. All applicants, however, had first to be nominated by an acceptable sponsor (fig. 1). If they were successful, they then underwent a rigorous rehearsal programme to prepare them for the great day, the most demanding moment of which, at least for the women, was endeavouring to back gracefully out of the room without tripping over their trains. Special clothes were required, and court dress always retained some fossilized elements of the fashions of the late eighteenth century, so that men wore knee breeches long after trousers had become universal for normal wear, and women continued to affect the long trains and high ostrich feather head-dresses of the 1790s (figs 1, 2 and 3). Although the experience was so eagerly sought after, it seems on the whole to have been rather trying. When John and Effie Ruskin were presented in 1850, John, although delighted and flattered by the honour bestowed on him, could not but deplore what he described as, 'the most awkward crush I ever saw in my life; the floor was covered with the ruins of ladies dresses, torn lace and fallen flowers'; while Effie was even less impressed:

We then entered the reception room where was a dense crowd of waving plumes and diamonds crushed as close as they could pack. I was fortunate in getting a seat which if I had not I am sure I would have fainted. Several ladies did and one went into dreadful hysteria and screamed and laughed like a lunatic. She was carried out. We stayed in this broiling but amusing condition for two hours, the heat was dreadful . . . . At length the doors opened and we slowly were wedged forward to the Tapestry room . . . . The Queen looked immensely stout and red but very calm. I kissed her hand which was fat and red too and made a reverence to the Prince and Duke of Kent and then somebody threw my train over my arm again.[1]

But once this ordeal had been weathered, there were plenty of more amusing pastimes for the upper classes to indulge in. Queen Victoria's was not a particularly brilliant court, and she herself, although fond enough of pretty things, had no great interest in fashion. However, the great aristocratic families kept the social round going as it always had, and after the Queen was widowed and her son had married the stylish Alexandra of Denmark, the Prince and Princess of Wales took over her role as leader of the *beau monde* (fig. 4).

High on the list of fashionable pursuits came sporting events, the Ascot races and Henley Regatta (figs 5, 6 and 7), providing venues for the rich and mighty to meet and enjoy themselves. There was also the Derby (figs 9, 10 and 11), an event which attracted not just the nobility but vast crowds from every walk of life. An American clergyman, witnessing the scene in 1840, observed that,

in the same group, or standing near each other, might have been seen high born ladies, servant girls, gypsies and the most worthless of the sex, all pressing forward in one broad extended ring to witness the races

and he concluded that,

it seemed as though there was here brought before me, in one concentrated and panoramic view, an exhibition of the world's varied allurements of sin.

This highly coloured and democratic ragbag was perfectly captured by William Frith in his painting *The Derby Day* of 1858 (fig. 9). The rich also enjoyed a whole round of balls, house parties and dinner parties – very much grander and more formal than today's gatherings, with dozens of guests and scores of dishes. Such occasions, as well as lunch and garden parties, all demanded a confident grasp of etiquette and special clothes. In her memoirs, Cynthia Asquith recalled that a weekend house party in the early 1900s necessitated an outfit for church complete with best hat, three evening dresses, three tea-gowns, two tweed costumes with accompanying shirts, several country hats and a whole array of shoes, gloves, shawls and jewellery.

Cultural pursuits

Queen Victoria, herself, was very different from her

Hanoverian predecessors or, for that matter, from her eldest son. She and Albert were deeply in love, which was unusual in a royal match, and they preferred the seclusion of Balmoral or Osborne to the life of the court, though they were no shirkers where public duty was concerned. Their interests ran to painting and classical music rather than drinking or card playing; they had both retained from their careful upbringings an earnest desire for self-improvement; and they were deeply committed to an ideal of family life, of which poor Victoria, particularly, had felt the want in childhood. This was an ideology which her middle-class subjects, more numerous and articulate than ever before, could and did enthusiastically embrace, dressing their own small sons in tartan, calling their offspring after the royal children, and expressing an interest in culture if only to assert their own gentility.

This thirst for education and the arts was epitomized by the Great Exhibition of 1851, which was largely Albert's brainchild. Two years earlier, speaking as President of the Society of Arts, he had urged that,

> now is the time to prepare for a Great Exhibition, an exhibition worthy of the greatness of this country; not merely national in its scope and benefits, but comprehensive of the whole world; and I offer myself to the public as their leader, if they are willing to assist in the undertaking.

This blend of chauvinism and instructiveness was peculiarly appealing to the Victorian public, and plans went ahead. The Exhibition was duly opened by the Queen – almost overcome with pride at Albert's achievement – on 1 May 1851 (fig. 16), and remained open until the following October. Tickets were priced at one pound, half-a-crown and one shilling, and secured admission on particular days. A profit of £150,000 was made, which was subsequently used to establish the South Kensington Museums. Altogether, the Exhibition was visited by over six million people; with the population of London standing at just over two million, it meant that twice that number of out-of-towners made the journey to come and see it, a fact which had a profound bearing on the development of railway excursion tickets. By no means all of them were prosperous or educated: the Dorset poet William Barnes ran into one of his local acquaintances there and based his poem 'John Bloom in London' on the encounter:

> When Lon'on vok did meäke a show
> O' their girt glassen house woone year,
> An' people went, bwoth high an' low,
> To zee the zight, vrom vur an' near,
> 'O well,' cried Bloom, 'why I've a right
> So well's the rest to zee the zight;
> I'll goo, an' teäke the raïl outright.'

The Exhibition's success led to follow-ups, notably the Manchester Art Treasures Exhibition (fig. 17), which was opened by the Prince Consort on 5 May 1857, and which was devoted to the fine, rather than the applied, arts. In 1860 another London exhibition was mooted, again to be sponsored by Albert, but while discussions were in progress he quite suddenly died of typhoid, in December 1861. Plans went ahead, nevertheless, and the exhibition opened on 1 May 1862; it attracted even more visitors than before (fig. 18), but inevitably its success was overshadowed by the Prince's death and by the outbreak of the Civil War in America, and it failed to make a profit. However, all these exhibitions succeeded in firing the nation's imagination and enthusiasm, and cultural pursuits were eagerly adopted as a sign both of gentility and of high moral purpose.

Family life and rites of passage

The royal couple's devotion to their family also had a tremendous influence on middle-class social life. Rites of passage had always been celebrated, but now they took on an almost mystical significance. Until now christenings had mostly consisted of a drinking bout between the proud father and his cronies, the baby being an absent pretext for the celebration and the mother still confined to her bed. Victoria's own christening had been a disastrously tense and unhappy occasion: for her own nine children she was determined to do better, and Albert too threw himself into the preparations, designing a special gilt font and taking a hand in the cake as well. During this time, babies began to be baptized slightly later after birth so that the mother could participate; brothers and sisters were included, the long white embroidered robe was established as the proper wear and the afternoon tea with elaborate cake became the correct form of celebration. Weddings (figs 21–25), which had previously been viewed primarily as business transactions, now became sentimentalized in deference to the Queen's conjugal felicity, and in society the white wedding, complete with orange blossom, tiered cake and honeymoon, came into fashion. A whole new mythology developed around the bride, who was seen half as heroine – this being the supreme moment in her life – and half as sacrificial victim. Lower down the social scale a very much more down-to-earth attitude prevailed, and many brides either wore their existing best dress or acquired a new one which then became their best for years to come (fig. 23).

Trollope, expanding on an idea of Thackeray's,

described married women in terms of parasite plants:

Alone they but spread themselves on the ground, and cower unseen in the dingy shade. But when they have found their firm supporter, how wonderful is their beauty.

Victoria herself, no shrinking violet when it came to ruling the country or getting her own way, felt that her relationship with Albert was fundamentally unnatural in that he should have been the undisputed master, and husbands up and down the land agreed wholeheartedly. The problem came when the 'firm supporter' was withdrawn. Aged only 42, Victoria went almost insane with grief when Albert died, and was determined that life had nothing left to offer her. She plunged into total mourning, abandoning not only colours but also any interest in changing styles; she continued to dress in this depressing and increasingly frumpish fashion for the remaining 40 years of her life (figs 26 and 27). In this, as in everything else, she became a pattern for her subjects, and, although few took it as far as she did, the etiquette of mourning became more formalized than ever before. Women were expected to go into deepest black on the demise of quite distant relatives, and these rules were even applied to children and babies: Victoria wrote quite sharply to her daughter in Prussia who had failed to put her five-month-old baby into mourning for its great-grandmother (fig. 28). Men, meanwhile, contented themselves with black clothes for funerals and a black armband to denote bereavement (fig. 31).

Social life in the cities

It was in both the dress and the social life of ordinary people that the Victorian age stood out from the past. Until the last century few could afford much in the way of special clothes, and occasions to wear them were scarce. Family celebrations and occasional feasts like Harvest Home, which arose out of the work of the community, were the only interruptions in a pattern of hard and unremitting toil. Sunday merely required cleanliness, and holidays were unknown. With the Industrial Revolution, two things changed.

First, owing to the enormous boom in the textile industries, clothes themselves became very much cheaper than ever before. For the first time in history, the working classes were able to emulate, albeit with inferior materials and often with something of a time-lag, the clothes worn by their betters. This process was further encouraged by the improvement in communications and the gradual increase in literacy, which resulted in a whole literature of fashion. Moreover, people who worked in the textile industries developed into a distinct class who, despite limited spending power, took a quasi-professional interest in the whole subject of clothes, a fact noted by Mrs Gaskell in *North and South*, and rather more disparagingly by a contributor to *The Lady's Companion* of 1858:

> *The Manchester or Birmingham factory girl buys a gay shawl on credit, wears it on Sunday, puts it in pawn on Monday morning, and takes it out again on Saturday night for another Sunday's wear, and so on, until she has wasted money that would have bought a good wardrobe.*

Secondly, the old country ways whereby families stayed together and social life was closely tied to the events of the farming year were superseded by the more impersonal arrangements of the cities. Here youth and energy commanded higher wages than age and experience, and young people could lead lives of relative freedom and independence. In Disraeli's *Sybil* the elderly Mrs Carey is dismayed at what she sees:

> *'I think the world is turned upside downwards in these parts. A brat like Mick Radley to live in a two-pair, with a wife and family, or as good, as he says; and this girl asks me to take a dish of tea with her and keeps house! Fathers and mothers goes for nothing', continued Mrs. Carey, as she took a very long pinch of snuff, and deeply mused. 'Tis the children gets the wages,' she added after a profound pause, 'and there it is.'* [2]

In the cities geographical proximity did not necessarily connote an identity of interest or a common culture, and it was some time before these began to be supplied by alternative bodies to the local community: churches, political organizations or, in some cases, employing firms. Colleges for working men started in the 1850s, and clubs from 1860 after the founding of the pioneering Working Men's Mutual Improvement and Recreation Society. The YMCA began in London as early as 1844, developing out of Bible-reading meetings; it soon became associated with social amenities and physical recreation as well, and quickly spread across the country (figs 36–38). Later in the century numbers of enthusiastic and charismatic clergymen and social workers, typified by Mrs Humphry Ward's creation, Robert Elsmere, saw conveying culture and education as important a part of their mission as preaching. Paternalistic firms such as the Quaker companies of Cadbury, Rowntree and Colman were genuinely concerned with the welfare of their employees, and offered them a whole range of social activities, from schools and sports clubs to bands and outings (figs 39–49). Not everybody appreciated these facilities, but to many they were a godsend. Disraeli puts both points of view in *Sybil* when Caroline is asked why she has left Mr Trafford's mill:

'And then I'm no scholar,' said the girl, 'and never could take to learning. And those Traffords had so many schools.
'Learning is better than house and land,' said Mrs. Carey, 'though I'm no scholar myself; but then, in my time, things was different. But young persons –'
'Yes,' said Mick; 'I don't think I could get through the day, if it wurno' for our Institute.'
'And what's that?' asked Mrs. Carey, with a sneer.
'The Shoddy-Court Literary and Scientific, to be sure,' said Mick; 'we have got fifty members, and take in three London papers; one Northern Star *and two* Moral Worlds.*'*[3]

The influence of the railways

Although many of those who organized recreations for the working classes had excellent intentions, there was also undoubtedly an element of fear involved, a desire to keep potentially troublesome young people off the streets, to channel dangerous energies and to forestall political unrest. Thomas Cook, one of the most successful Victorian entrepreneurs, began modestly enough in 1841 when he liaised with the Midland Counties Railway to offer a cheap excursion ticket to a temperance meeting. He had been quick to perceive how spectacularly the development of the railways could alter the social life of the nation, making travel for pleasure a real possibility for even the poorest. The rich continued to take their holidays abroad, whether on the beaches of the south of France, in the Swiss mountains or on one of Cook's own foreign tours (fig. 54), but the less exalted could now escape from the polluted and insanitary cities and get to Ramsgate or Skegness, if not for a fortnight's holiday, then at least for a day's excursion (fig. 55). Going to the seaside became a national institution long before people started to enjoy swimming: it was the fresh air, the change of scene, the romantic possibilities and the carnival atmosphere that appealed (figs 59–65).

Exercise and sport

Along with this new mobility went a steady expansion in sporting activities for both men and women throughout the second half of the nineteenth century. The overcrowding of the cities, and in particular the outbreaks of cholera of 1849 and 1866, had prompted concern for public health and led to the beginnings of sanitary legislation. Now the importance of exercise was stressed, unnecessarily in the country where farm boys played cricket on the village green and even highborn ladies walked for miles, but crucially in towns where there were no natural facilities for such things.

Happily, the pursuit of health could also afford interesting social opportunities, and sports like archery, croquet and tennis were avidly seized upon as chances to meet and mingle with the opposite sex. Croquet did not demand special clothes, though it did give rise to a rather fetching fashion for looping up the skirt of the petticoat – in theory to clear the path for the mallet. The earliest tennis costumes however, were designed with no apparent thought for the practicalities of the game; they therefore conformed to the fashions of the day with tight-fitting bodices and bustled skirts, the only concession to functionalism being an apron worn over the dress with a pocket for spare balls (fig. 71). Whether the game was viewed seriously as a sport can be gauged from the remark in an etiquette book of the 1880s that the terms 'garden-party' and 'lawn-tennis party' were virtually interchangeable; but clearly the romantic potential was not always realized, for the same writer concludes somewhat forlornly that,

in some remote counties the gentlemen . . . are represented by three or four young curates and two or three old gentlemen, while the ladies present muster from 40 to 50, in which case very little wine is drunk.

The Hockey Association was formed in 1886, and by 1900 it was far and away the most popular winter game for schoolgirls (fig. 73). Mixed hockey was also a favourite pastime, largely for the reason given by *Punch* in this poem of 1903:

And today I'm so excited that I feel inclined to scream
  But a certain sense of modesty prevails
For this very afternoon I am to play against a team
  That will be composed of eligible males.
    Though I do not care two pins
    Which side loses, or which wins,
I may get some introductions if I hit 'em on the shins.

The bicycle and the motor car

But it was the bicycle, more than anything else, which transformed Victorian life, opening up new horizons and setting completely new standards in personal mobility. Initially, it was viewed with disapproval and derision, so that the earliest cyclists banded together in clubs to enhance their confidence (fig. 76). The Victorians took it seriously, as was their wont, and debated earnestly what were the proper clothes for this exhilarating but exacting new sport. The problem lay in combining comfort and practicality with a truly feminine modesty, and the knickerbockers adopted by a few brave souls were never totally accepted. In 1893 *Etiquette of Good Society* ruled that ladies should wear:

a plain skirt, made sufficiently wide to allow the feet full play without causing them to draw up the dress by their action, and yet not so wide as to permit the skirt to hang in folds or flap in the wind. A Norfolk jacket, made to fit neatly but not too neatly to the figure, cut low round the throat to allow the neck free action. Both skirt and jacket should be made of a woollen material, and one that is porous and of little weight. A soft silk handkerchief is worn round the neck, which will hide the absence of collar and brooch. Shoes, having firm but heavy soles, and a close-fitting soft hat made of the same material as the dress, complete the costume. The dress of a gentleman is knickerbockers, and a short coat buttoned up the front; stockings ribbed and knitted of thick wool; shoes with stout soles; and a cap with peaks at the front and back, made like the suit, of porous woollen material, or an ordinary straw hat. A light silk handkerchief loosely tied round the neck should take the place of a stiff collar.

The popularity of cycling increased so rapidly that it soon became a truly classless occupation. *Punch* carried numerous jokes about servants demanding parking space for their bicycles, and Flora Thompson, remembering the excitement and amusement with which the villagers of Lark Rise rushed out to watch the cycling clubs go by, remarked how incredulous they would have been had they known,

that in a few years there would be at least one bicycle in every one of their houses, that the men would ride to work on them and the younger women, when their housework was done, would lightly mount 'the old bike' and pedal away to the market town to see the shops.[4]

But by that time the recreational aspect of cycling had been overtaken by its function as a means of transport, and special clothes were no longer needed.

Exactly the same process operated with motoring. Because of its expense, for a long time it was restricted to the rich, and the low speeds and frequent breakdowns of early motor cars meant again that it was seen more as a pleasant pastime than as an efficient way to travel. Also, until cars appeared in any great numbers, the roads they travelled on were not surfaced; motor vehicles, therefore, threw up a huge amount of dust and mud and made protective clothing a necessity. Goggles and duster coats were worn, and women added hats with veils that completely covered their faces (figs 80–82).

Children's clothes

Children were seldom able to enjoy their best clothes. By modern standards they were generally grossly over-dressed, especially in summer, and their clothes were not designed for comfort but to show off their parents' status. Among the poorer classes this meant chiefly a very high standard of cleanliness, expressed in the whiteness and stiffness of collars and pinafores – the starch repelled dirt as well as preserving the shape of the garment. Among the wealthy it meant clothes which approximated closely to adult fashions, however inappropriate: bustles for little girls, top hats for boys. Alternatively, outfits embodied a parental fantasy: highland dress or sailor suits (figs 88–90). None of these things were calculated to appeal to the children themselves. C. S. Lewis feelingly described his transition from play clothes to formal school uniform:

Only this morning – only two hours ago – I was running wild in shorts and blazer and sandshoes. Now I am choking and sweating, itching too, in thick dark stuff, throttled by an Eton collar, my feet already aching with unaccustomed boots. I am wearing knickerbockers that button at the knee. Every night for some forty weeks of every year and for many a year I am to see the red, smarting imprint of those buttons in my flesh when I undress. Worst of all is the bowler-hat, apparently made of iron, which grasps my head.[5]

Little girls did not fare much better, despite the ostensible prettiness and softness of their best dresses, because these were offset by the grim nature of their undergarments. Eleanor Farjeon recalled how her delight in a new salmon-pink surah dress with cream silk trimmings was mitigated by the:

stiff, scratchy petticoats that were one of the minor tortures of my life. So was the hat elastic, which left a red mark under my chin, and when slipped behind my ears for relief, made my head ache. So were the tight little kid gloves worked down my fingers till I could get my thumb in. So were the bronze boots now being buttoned over two pairs of stockings, cashmere underneath and silk on top, so that I shouldn't take cold; because of this my insteps were pinched, and my feet were icy.[6]

But if all children dreaded Sunday best, the worst humiliation was reserved for those with artistic mothers, who used their children as a means to indulge romantic fantasies. To be dressed as a little Scotsman, or a miniature able-seaman, was one thing, but to be togged up in black velvet knee breeches and lace collars, and perhaps, worse still, to be forced to wear one's hair in ringlets, was more than most Victorian boys could bear with equanimity (figs 91–93). But if their mothers had read and loved Frances Hodgson Burnett's *Little Lord Fauntleroy*, such was their fate. The six-year-old Compton Mackenzie suffered so much from the mockery of the other boys at his dancing class that he threw himself down into the gutter on the way there, cutting the breeches and tearing the collar, and rendering the whole outfit unwearable. He thus avoided being photographed in what he called 'that infernal get-up!'.

Conclusion

In addition to regular social engagements and recreational activities, there was a vast range of occasions for which the Victorians and Edwardians enjoyed dressing up: outings to the theatre, music hall or picture palace; river trips; agricultural shows and village fêtes; openings of buildings; award-giving ceremonies; celebrations of public events such as the Queen's Jubilee; and countless others. But although the range was great, it is important to keep a perspective. Our forebears worked, by and large, very much harder and for longer hours than we do; their holidays were brief, rare and precious and their leisure time strictly limited. Because of this, they were determined to extract the maximum

enjoyment from every occasion, and to do full sartorial justice to it. Our own relaxed and informal approach to dress would have shocked them deeply. Alison Uttley beautifully captures this sense of creating an occasion in *The Country Child*, when she describes a prosperous farmer's family setting off to see a travelling circus at the end of the nineteenth century:

The milking was over early, and Dan washed his face and polished it with a cloth till it shone like one of the apples. He changed his corduroys to Sunday trousers, and put on a blue and white collar. He dipped his brush in the lading-can, and sleeked his hair in front of the flower-wreathed little glass. Then, after harnessing the pony in the best pony trap, he left her with a rug on her back, and walked down the hill, with a Glory rose pinned in his cap and a spray of lad's love in his button-hole, to take the field path over the mountain to Broomy Vale.

Mrs Garland wore her purple velvet bonnet trimmed with pansies, which Susan loved and admired so much. She drew a little spotted veil over her face and peeped through like a robin in a cage.

Susan's eyes shone out from under her grey serge hat, which her mother had made and trimmed with the soft feathers from a pheasant's breast. She, too, looked like a bird, an alarmed, excited, joyful hedge-sparrow, as she hopped up and down. On her shoulders she wore the grey cape with a grey fur edge which she wore for school, old-fashioned and homely, lined with scarlet flannel to keep her warm, and this flapped like a pair of wings . . . .

Becky polished up the trap lamps, and put in fresh candles. Then Tom Garland came downstairs in his Sunday clothes, smelling of lavender, with his horseshoe tie-pin in the spotted silk tie, and a silk handkerchief peeping from his breast pocket. Margaret looked up at him proudly, he was the best-looking man in England, she thought, and Susan put her hand in his.[7]

References

1 Admiral Sir William James, *The Order of Release*, John Murray, 1947, pp. 159–60.

2 Benjamin Disraeli, *Sybil*, 1845, 9th edition, Oxford World's Classics, 1969, pp. 91–2.

3 Disraeli, op. cit., p. 90.

4 Flora Thompson, *Over to Candleford*, Oxford, 1941, 4th edition, Penguin, 1974, p. 255.

5 C. S. Lewis, *Surprised by Joy*, Geoffrey Bles, 1955, p. 29.

6 Eleanor Farjeon, *A Nursery in the Nineties*, Gollancz, 1935; Oxford, 1980, p. 339.

7 Alison Uttley, *The Country Child*, Faber, 1931; Penguin, 1966, pp. 61–2. (By kind permission of Faber & Faber.)

1 Elsie Mary Buckle in presentation dress, c. 1897

Elsie Mary Buckle was an Admiral's daughter from Lincolnshire, born in 1879. She was presented at court in 1897, and her sponsor for the occasion was Lady Rawlinson. Here, she can be seen wearing the statutary long train and an ostrich feather head-dress; elbow-length gloves, a string of pearls round her neck, and a large bouquet complete the outfit. Her front hair is also of the period, arranged in the curly fringe popularized by Princess Alexandra.

2 Mrs Arthur Lee and Miss Faith Moore in presentation dress, c. 1905

These two sisters were American heiresses. Their dresses and trains are elaborately embroidered and spangled; the bodices have the pouched effect characteristic of the early Edwardian period. They wear necklaces and carry ribboned bouquets and their hair is rolled back over pads away from their faces and surmounted by the traditional cluster of ostrich feathers.

3 Sir John Cameron Lamb in ceremonial dress, c. 1905–10

Born in 1845, Sir John Cameron Lamb was made a Companion of St Michael and St George in 1890, a Companion of the Bath in 1895, and knighted in 1905. He became Second Secretary of the Post Office, and in 1903 travelled to Berlin as Senior British Delegate to the first World Conference on Wireless Telegraphy.

On this occasion he is wearing the cut-in tail coat which had been adopted for dress wear at the beginning of the nineteenth century, with heavy gilt embroidery on the high-standing collar and cuffs; white breeches buttoned at the knee; white silk stockings with a decorative motif or 'clock' up the ankle; and flat pumps. He carries a sword and plumed hat, and wears his decorations.

4 Edward Prince of Wales and Alexandra of Denmark on their wedding day, 10 March 1863

Queen Victoria was still in heavy mourning for Albert who had died fifteen months earlier, when her eldest son married. Although she appeared at the wedding in black and insisted that the ladies of her court should wear shades of half-mourning — lilac and grey — she did not succeed in dampening the general mood of celebration. Bertie's pleasure-loving nature and Alix's natural elegance and grace assured their popularity with the public and established them as leaders of an 'alternative' court at Marlborough House. The 19-year-old Princess's dress is of white satin trimmed with orange blossom and myrtle, with a veil of Honiton lace, held in place by a wreath. Her hair falls in ringlets and she wears ear-rings. Beside her stands the 22-year-old Prince, wearing the uniform of a General and the ceremonial robes of the Order of the Garter.

5 Henley, c. 1895

The men are mostly dressed in light flannel trousers and either blazers or shirt sleeves; boaters are ubiquitous. The ladies have the large leg-of-mutton sleeves characteristic of this period. Since suntans are still considered vulgar they carry sunshades, most of them curved like umbrellas, but one or two of the flat Japanese-type.

6 Henley, c. 1903

A very different view of Henley, and one which perfectly conjures up the fabled long hot summers of the Edwardian age. The ladies are immaculately dressed in white dresses and large hats, and exude poise and assurance. The gentlemen wear the inevitable boater. The whole picture is suggestive of leisure and privilege.

7 Ascot, 1900

The Ascot Races were one of the high points of the social year. Safe within the Royal Enclosure, the privileged could enjoy being stared at and admired by the crowds. Formal dress was de rigueur. The men are in morning dress with top hats and light gloves, and all carry binoculars. The lady in the foreground looks strikingly simple in her self-coloured costume; the other ladies are more typical in wearing light and frothy dresses with matching parasols and large, heavily-trimmed hats.

8 Black Ascot, 1910

After the death of Edward VII in May 1910, mourning dress was adopted on a wide scale, but after the first few weeks the social round continued unabated. This picture illustrates how, even within the strict limits of mourning etiquette, fashion could be enthusiastically followed.

9 The Derby Day, by William Powell Frith, 1858

The Derby was the closest that England came to a carnival, and Frith's painting captures the uninhibited social mixture of the event. 'In the same throng,' commented an American visitor a few years earlier, 'pressing forward to gaze upon the exciting spectacle, were the gentry and the very offscouring of the earth, clad in rags and squalidness'. Prosperous couples and beggars, fashionable ladies and acrobats, countrymen up for a day's excitement and emaciated flower-sellers, can all be seen here.

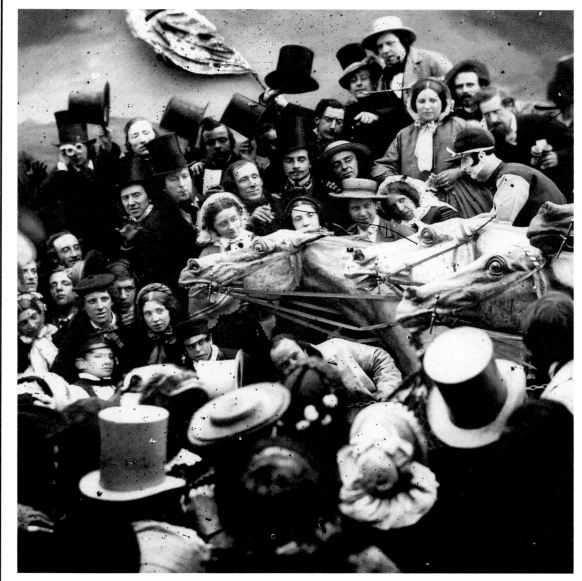

10 A racecourse scene, c. 1859

This rather comic studio photograph is apparently intended to show a Derby crowd. The onlookers show their excitement by pressing right up to the racing wooden horses and waving their top hats in the air.

11 The Derby, 1911

Another picture illustrating the dictum that men are all equal only on the turf or under it. A motley group has gathered on a taxicab and is watching the finish with tense expressions. On the left are a team of bookmakers, one holding the book and the other the money-bag. The two men in caps and duster coats are chauffeurs. The young man is of a distinctly higher social class than the four ladies, one of whom seems to be having trouble seeing out from under her hat.

12 A house party at Crichel More, Dorset, November 1894

Posed group photographs like this one were a common feature of society house parties. The seated man in the double-breasted overcoat is the Prince of Wales. The gentlemen are in informal country dress – soft caps, loose jackets and knickerbockers, thick knitted stockings and boots; the man on the extreme right wears puttees. The ladies, in contrast, are very elegantly turned out in well-fitting coats, furs, tight gloves and smart hats. The Prince sits between the two prettiest.

13 A house party, early 1890s

*Mr and Mrs Jeremiah James Colman of Norwich entertain Mr and Mrs Gladstone (centre) at The Clyffe, their
seaside home near Lowestoft. This is not a society house party, and the clothes, in particular the caps worn by Mrs
Gladstone and Mrs Colman, bespeak solid middle class respectability rather than fashion.*

14 A luncheon party at Ritters Hotel, Homburg, 1910

The hosts were Judge Short and Sir William Russell. The gentlemen are, on the whole, informally dressed in lounge suits, soft-collared shirts and knotted ties; some of them have flowers in their buttonholes. The ladies are in smart day dresses with high necks and long sleeves, and all wear fashionably large hats, some of which could almost be confused with the table decorations. The waiters wear black tail coats, white waistcoats and bow ties.

15 The Wedding Morning, by Lock, 1840

Victoria and Albert on their wedding day, 10 February 1840. The Queen and her Consort represented the epitome of conjugal bliss to their subjects, and this painting shows them as Victoria liked to think of them: the noble and earnest husband inspiring and guiding his submissive wife.

Victoria's wedding dress was of white satin trimmed with a thousand pound's worth of Honiton lace. She wears a veil and wreath, a necklace and dangling ear-rings, and carries a bouquet. Her hair is smoothed down, parted in the middle and looped over her ears. Albert is in ceremonial dress: a dress coat with magnificent epaulettes, white breeches, silk stockings and buckled pumps. He carries a pair of white gloves, and his hair is carefully waved. Both wear the Order of the Garter.

16 The Opening of the Great Exhibition, 1 May 1851

For what she later called 'the happiest, proudest day of my life' Victoria wore a dress of pink watered silk, embroidered with silver and diamonds, and a head-dress of feathers and jewels. Albert is in uniform. Their eldest son Bertie stands next to his mother, wearing Highland costume, and on his other side stands his sister Vicky, in a low-cut flounced dress of some flimsy embroidered fabric. The men in the foreground are in a variety of uniforms, some of them a direct throw-back to the eighteenth century with their knee breeches, cravats and embroidered waistcoats, but most of them in trousers cut so long as to cover most of the foot, and kept taut by a strap under the instep. From the figures in the background it is difficult to pick out much beyond a great many bonnets, and shawls hung over the edge of the balcony.

17 The opening of the Manchester Art Treasures Exhibition, 5 May 1857

The Prince Consort performs the opening ceremony at the Manchester Art Treasures Exhibition. The exhibition which ran for five and a half months, was seen by 1,300,000 people, and has been called 'the outstanding British artistic occasion of the nineteenth century'.

The ladies are conspicuous for their mostly light-coloured flounced dresses, off-the-face bonnets and pyramidal outline, whilst the gentlemen are uniformly dark and vertical: the contrast between men's and women's appearance has seldom been greater than at this time.

18 The Majolica Fountain at the International Exhibition, 1862

Eight of the 6,117,450 visitors to the Exhibition having a rest. The ladies are in fashionable day dress. Their 'spoon-shaped' bonnets are tied with very wide strings, and their skirts — the one in the middle of corded watered silk — are held out by crinolines. They all have tight-fitting gloves and smooth, centre-parted hair. The lady on the left has a black lace shawl. The gentlemen all appear to be in dark suits, with or without top hats, with the exception of the figure on the right whose facial hair, informal clothes and 'wideawake' hat suggest an artistic bent. The standing figure in a shiny-buttoned coat and top hat is perhaps an Exhibition attendant.

19 Dorchester Vocal Association Concert, c. 1900

The concert was held in the corn exchange, which was suitably decorated with potted palms and swags of fabric. With four exceptions, the ladies are all in pale dresses, mostly high-necked, and all of them have their hair rolled and padded away from their faces. The lady to the left of the conductor appears, from the square band of trimming at her neck and the general cut of her dress, to have aesthetic leanings. The gentlemen are in evening dress with starched shirt fronts.

20 A christening, c. 1860

For this christening, the baby wears a long white robe, the embroidered and scalloped hem of which reaches almost to the ground, and the gentlemen are both in dark suits. Being in church, the men have removed their top hats. The ladies have fashionable 'spoon-shaped' bonnets with broad strings, flounced dresses worn over crinolines, mantles and gloves. (The Ladies Treasury of 1857 ruled that only the imminent danger of fainting could justify removing one's gloves in church.) The girls have shorter skirts and hats with turned-down brims and feather trimming.

21 A wedding in the Colman family, c. 1888

Jeremiah James Colman of Norwich and his wife Caroline are the two figures immediately to the right of the bridal group. This may be the wedding of their son Russell to Edith M. Davies, which took place in 1888. All the women carry magnificent bouquets. The bridesmaids wear the fashionable 'postboy' hats, their height augmented by the vertical flower trimming; with their full draped skirts this gives them a curiously pyramidal look.

22 A wedding, c. 1894

The poor bride appears somewhat eclipsed by the exuberant hats and sleeves of her female guests. Hats like these were fastened to the coiffure with long sharp pins; Gwen Raverat remembered bitterly how in windy weather 'their mighty sails flapped agonizingly at their anchorage, and pulled out one's hair by the handful'. The little bridesmaid's artistic frock and frilled bonnet look rather at odds with her severe hairstyle.

23 A country wedding, c. 1910

In this country wedding in the village of Holford, the bride was a farmer's daughter and the bridegroom a gardener. The young women at the right and left of the picture are the bride's married sisters; the baby is her niece; and the older woman her mother. All the participants have clearly taken a great deal of trouble with their appearance, but not surprisingly the women's dresses are at least five years out of date by fashionable standards. Indeed, the sister on the right is wearing her own wedding dress of a few years before, which illustrates how much longer styles persist in real life than in fashion magazines.

24 A bridesmaid, 1911

For the wedding celebrated here at Brompton Oratory, the bridegroom was Viscount Gormanston and the bride was the daughter of General Sir William and Lady Elizabeth Butler, the painter of military scenes. This particular bridesmaid was an art student, and usually somewhat bohemian in her style of dress. Lady Butler (her aunt) wrote privately to her mother:

> Poor Olivia, she will not be altogether happy wearing the Philistine dress in (as you warrant) *a Philistine way* but *you* will think the dresses simply enchanting . . . . Poor Olivia, she will have to obey her mother and get into corsets (ugh!) for the fitting & she must *not* wriggle out of them for the great occasion!

Olivia retaliated by posing for the group photograph with her bouquet held down in a deliberately offhand way, while the other four bridesmaids held theirs up at conventional waist level.

25 A clerical wedding, 1914

The wedding of Mary Helen Barbara Moule and Thomas Cutler des Barres, a clergyman. She was 38 and he was 47. Perhaps she felt that a white dress would look inappropriately girlish, so she is dressed in a very plain coat and skirt, brightened up by a feathered hat and a beautiful large bouquet. None of the ladies present could be called elegant, though they have all made efforts with their hats. A good many of the male guests are clergymen.

26 Queen Victoria, c. 1870

This informal picture of the widowed Queen shows her outside with a companion. Her white cap frames her face and over it she wears a black silk hood trimmed with jet beads. A cloak, also trimmed with jet, hangs over the back of her seat. She holds a bunch of flowers and gazes abstractedly into the distance. The striped parasol probably belongs to her companion.

27 Queen Victoria, c. 1875

By this date Albert had been dead for 14 years, but Victoria is still in deep mourning. Her black crape-trimmed dress has a white collar and undersleeves, she wears a locket round her neck on a black ribbon, and a white widow's cap with long streamers. Not only the depth of her mourning, but the style of her clothes, has remained virtually unchanged over the years, emphasizing her complete withdrawal from the world.

28 The Crown Princess of Prussia and her children, 1861

This portrait of Vicky, Queen Victoria's eldest daughter, was taken on 1 December 1861, less than a fortnight before Prince Albert's death. The Princess is presumably wearing black for some more distant relative, but she has taken her mother's strictures to heart and included her children in her mourning. The two-year-old Willy wears a black dress with a pleated skirt and a black sash, and the baby Victoria has her white dress and cap trimmed with black ribbons.

29 The Hon. Mrs Ponsonby and Bettie, c. 1860

The baby in this picture appears to be in mourning. Mrs Ponsonby's black silk dress, trimmed with bands of watered silk and finished off by a plain white collar, is certainly sombre, but the absence of crape would make it unacceptable for any serious degree of mourning. The baby, on the other hand, is swathed in a white gauze shawl with a deep black border. A possible explanation is that they are not mother and child, as the pose would suggest, but that Mrs Ponsonby was a friend of the baby's dead mother.

(previous page)
30 A mourning group, 1906–7

This is a studio portrait, presumably taken to commemorate a family death. The women are all in deepest black. The dresses are not in the height of fashion, and not one of them is trimmed with crape, which was still at this time the traditional fabric of mourning. The women are also wearing tight gloves and heavily trimmed and feathered hats. The child wears a coat with a wide shoulder cape and a bonnet, both white, which was an acceptable mourning colour for very young children.

31 A funeral at Stratford-On-Avon, 1899

Here the men manage to look funereal simply by putting on their best clothes. They hold their top hats or bowlers in their hands. In contrast, the women are in ordinary outdoor dress, not necessarily black, and are mostly wearing boaters.

44

32 The oldest inhabitants of West Ilsley, c. 1895

This picture by Henry Taunt illustrates the sense of local group identity found in country places. The men at either end of the line wear the traditional garb of the countryman: loose jackets, trousers, soft hats and stout boots – the man on the far right has his laces undone. Everybody else is manifestly in their Sunday best. The women cling to the now unfashionable bonnets of their younger days, with crocheted shawls for added warmth.

33 A decorated farm waggon, early twentieth century

This waggon won first prize in a harvest festival at Bursted, Hampshire. Social life in the country has always revolved around the sequence of the agricultural year, with events like sheep-shearing, threshing or butchering providing the pretext for celebrations and binding the community together.

46 Colmans' Employees Gymnastics Club, 1908

The boys all wear white cotton shirts, except for one who has a long-sleeved knitted vest. They have mostly light-coloured flannel trousers held up by belts or cummerbunds, dark socks and light soft shoes.

47 Carrow school infants' department, c. 1900

This school clearly owes a lot to the kindergarten movement which had started in the 1880s. The smaller children have a Noah's Ark to play with and feel quite proprietorial about the animals, while the older ones are occupied with different crafts including basket-weaving and modelling. Many of the children have rolled up their sleeves and all wear protective aprons. Some of the children are very young – the little boy in the front row third from the left is still in a dress.

48 Carrow school girls' department, 1890s

The girls look more cheerful than is usual in school groups of this period, so perhaps the happy and creative atmosphere of the infants' class continued higher up the school. They are all wearing dark dresses which look at first sight like a uniform, but are in fact amazingly varied in cut and construction, some being quite artistic. Perhaps they were the products of a needlework class.

49 A garden party for Colmans' employees, 25 July 1914

The party, for women and girls employed at Carrow works, was held in the grounds of Carrow Abbey. The event included dancing to a band, games, singing, recitations, magic tricks, teas and ices. The fashionable excesses of the Edwardian age, the huge flower-laden hats and elaborate blouses, have given way to an uncluttered, tubular look. These women in their plain coats and skirts, their simple round straw hats encircled with black, look almost as though they were in uniform. This, together with the total absence of men, gives the picture, taken on the eve of the Great War, a curiously prophetic quality.

50 London & North Western Railway Coventry Athletics Team, 1910

No doubt they looked more impressive in action, for it must be admitted that, posed as they are, with their ill-fitting vests, long crumpled shorts and wrinkled socks, the members of the athletics team look decidedly inferior to their two uniformed colleagues.

51 Whitby Bros staff outing, c. 1900

The employees of a Yeovil printing firm having a day out at Batcombe Down. All of them are wearing three-piece suits; all but four have moustaches. It is in their choice of headgear that they express their individuality. Eight are bareheaded, and the others sport soft caps, bowlers, boaters, trilbys and one panama. The ferocious-looking character on the extreme right of the second row from the back wears a strange hybrid which adds to his exotic air. (A printing firm outing is traditionally known as a wayzgoose.*)*

52 The Dorset County Chronicle staff picnic, 14 July 1906

The group is posed against the cliffs at West Lulworth. Nearly all of the men wear suits, with a variety of headgear — boaters and soft caps predominate, but there are one or two trilbys and panamas as well. Most of the women are wearing the ubiquitous full-sleeved white blouse and plain dark skirt, though a few are in dresses or costumes. They mostly have elaborately trimmed hats, but the two on the extreme right have opted for the flat tweed caps which were associated with sport. How, wearing those skirts, they have got as far up the cliff as they have, is a mystery.

53 Lucy Walker, c. 1860

The fragile, timid Victorian maiden of fiction was not nearly so common as is often supposed. Few, however, were as dauntless as Lucy Walker. At a time when many well-to-do families holidayed in the Swiss mountains, she surpassed them all by scaling the Matterhorn. This picture of Lucy, her companion and two local guides was probably taken in a studio, but it shows the type of clothes which she really wore for her exploit, and which made no obvious concessions to practicality: a full-skirted dress of checked fabric, probably wool, a hat, and stout shoes. Her companion wears an informal check jacket and waistcoat, trousers tucked into thick socks, and a felt hat with a scarf round the crown.

Paris-Motor-Car Excursions - TH. COOK & FILS

54 A Cooks tour of Paris, c. 1905

*The rich had always holidayed abroad. Thomas Cook's success lay in making foreign travel available to the middle
classes in an unthreatening form. In this promotional picture he is offering 'two hours' rides round Paris and its environs'
in a motorized char-a-banc. One of the ladies in the party is conspicuous in her white dress and large hat and veil; the
other, three rows behind her, is virtually indistinguishable from the gentlemen in her cloth costume and sensible felt hat.*

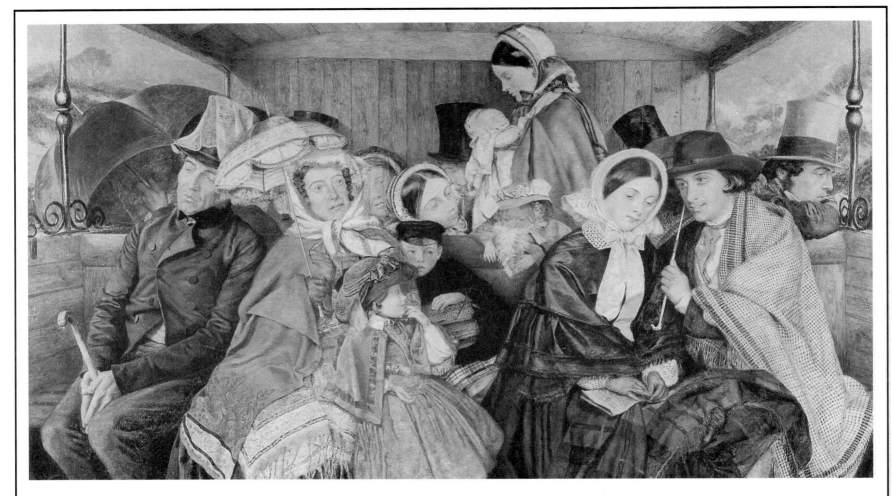

55 To Brighton and back for 3/6d, by Charles Rossiter, 1859

Cheap railway travel transformed the nation's holiday habits, enabling, in Ruskin's famous phrase, 'every fool in Buxton [to] be at Bakewell in half-an-hour, and every fool in Bakewell at Buxton'. The occupants of this compartment seem to be suffering from overcrowding, and have made matters worse by putting up their parasols.

56 Paddington Station during the Railway Strike, 1911

The strike lasted for two days, 18–19 August. This waiting crowd includes resigned businessmen as well as frustrated holidaymakers.

57 Waiting for the train, c. 1905–10

A middle class family setting out on their holidays from Paddington. The ladies are in town clothes, but the children are already in holiday get-up. The two older boys are in jerseys, knickerbockers, stockings and lace-up shoes while the youngest has bare legs and sandals. The eldest wears a boater; the other two have soft straw hats with turned-down brims. All three have their hair cut very short.

58 The beach at Ramsgate, c. 1870

The Victorians were neither sun-worshippers nor lovers of salt water. For them, the chief attraction of the seaside was that it presented an opportunity to see and to be seen. All the people in this picture are determinedly well covered up, and they sit on their hard chairs ignoring the sand and protecting themselves from whatever sun may be shining. The standing couple in the foreground look singularly out of place to modern eyes: he in his frock coat and top hat, she in her stylish striped silk dress, lace fichu and pork-pie hat. The girls sitting in the centre of the picture ostensibly reading or sewing wear their hair falling loose down their backs. This was a fashion restricted to the seaside, and a brisk trade in false switches consequently went on at coastal resorts.

59 On the pier, Hampshire, c. 1870

Here again, the subjects' clothes have been chosen for style rather than practicality. The ladies wear dresses with elaborate skirt drapery; the two in the foreground have flat 'Dolly Varden' hats tilted forward over their large chignons. The two young men lounging against the railing are in tail coats and top hats; the man with the dog wears a less formal lounge jacket and bowler; and the bearded book-lover strolls along in a loose paletot and a wideawake hat. All the subjects have the self-conscious air of those who know they are being scrutinized.

Note the bathing machines drawn up to the right of the picture.

60 A fashion plate: Le Journal des Enfants, August, 1886

It is difficult to believe that even an artist could have seriously suggested dressing children for the beach in clothes like these. One can only hope that parents had more common sense. The child on the extreme right is prudently heading away from the sea as fast as she can, doubtless anxious to preserve her high-heeled shoes, but some of the others are courting disaster by settling themselves, Canute-like, right in the path of the oncoming waves. Two of them have even pushed recklessness to the point of getting their feet wet.

Two of the boys wear versions of the sailor suit, which has a certain logic, but the choice of Highland costume for the third seems wholly whimsical. The youngest girl has fared best with her short, sleeveless frock; her two older companions are hopelessly bundled up, and recall Gwen Raverat's cousins who took off their boots and stockings on a hot day in order to paddle, and were made to put them straight back on again.

61 Porthminster Beach, Cornwall, c. 1900

By now people are beginning to get into the spirit of the seaside a little more. Bathing machines have been replaced by changing huts which can be wheeled down to the water's edge, and deck chairs have appeared. One or two groups are even sitting on rugs on the sand. The men are dressed in suits or blazers and flannels, the women in blouses and skirts; all have hats.

62 A family group on the beach, c. 1905

Three generations are enjoying a seaside picnic. The quantity of clothes they are wearing is directly related to their age. The grandparents have made no concessions whatever to the occasion. She is swathed in black, caped and bonneted; he sits stiffly in his tidy suit and bowler hat. The younger women are all hatless and, with one exception, coatless, while of the two younger men one at least wears his coat open and sports a boater. The little boys are bare-headed and bare-legged, and wear simple shirts and shorts.

63 *A fashion plate from* Le Follet, *1876*

This picture perfectly illustrates the divergence between fashion and practicality which has already been commented on. Nothing less suitable for boating could be imagined than these stylish, elaborately draped and flounced costumes, complete with ribboned hats and parasols, and worn over tight corsets. The only concession to the holiday spirit is in the long, flowing 'back hair' of the model on the right, an informal style much in favour at the seaside.

64 The beach at Skegness, 1909

By now the beach has become a lively place indeed, with icecream stalls, a photographic studio and a helter-skelter. The varied crowd includes a baby in a pushchair, bare-legged children with buckets and spades, boys in jerseys and knickerbockers, seamen with rolled-up trousers and nautical caps, and muffled-up elderly ladies.

65 Children on the beach, 1909

The children wear a variety of outfits. The two on the right have simply tucked up the skirts of their rather unsuitable dresses. The child in the middle wears a wide hat, an ordinary sailor top and dark baggy knickers. The two on the left wear carefully designed outfits consisting of shorts and jerseys with matching pull-on hats. The little girl standing just behind the line wears a loose square-necked smock and has a round hat dangling at her shoulders.

66 A lady on horseback, c. 1880

Upper-class Victorian ladies were expected to be good horsewomen, and most were, owing to the amount of time they spent on their country estates. As it was required that they should ride side-saddle, riding habits were intricately cut to fall in graceful folds whilst concealing the raised knee beneath. This lady has completed her outfit with a jaunty little felt hat, and gloves, perhaps of doeskin. The groom wears a frock coat with shiny buttons, short pale trousers, a top hat and boots. The little boy lounging in the gateway appears to be wearing a velvet knickerbocker suit with a deep white collar and cuffs, and his hair is in ringlets.

67 Young archers, 1858

Archery was considered as suitable for women as it was for men, prompting, as George Eliot observed, 'attitudes full of grace and power'. The young people here wear a surprising variety of dress, ranging from the formal top hat and morning coat of the boy in the centre to the scruffy suit, with a makeshift belt round the waist, of the boy at the extreme right. The girls wear short, full skirts over crinolines and loose-sleeved jackets. The one in the centre has a stylish pork-pie hat trimmed with a feather. The older couple sit in rather fancy garden chairs.

**68 and 69   Lady Beatrix and The Hon. George
Lambton in riding dress, 1860s**

*Boys and girls were dressed in the same style of clothes until they were about
five. These two wear identical riding dresses of check cloth trimmed with
braid. The bodices fasten with buttons down the front, the sleeves are close-
fitting to the wrist and the full skirts are pleated. They have matching jackets
and white collars, and wear short white socks and boots, his fastening with
laces and hers with buttons. The only difference between them is in their hats,
the length of their hair and the fact that she sits side-saddle.*

70 A group of young people, c. 1865

This picture captures the flirtatious atmosphere which surrounded the playing of croquet. The two young women in the middle were the sisters of W. S. Gilbert. Their hair is drawn back into chignons, and their plain dresses and bare heads suggest that they are on home ground while the other two, more obviously dressed-up young women, are perhaps visitors. The young men are in informal day dress.

71 A garden scene, early 1880s

A doctor's family enjoying a peaceful afternoon in their Hertfordshire garden. The father is in formal day clothes; the mother wears a dress in the style of the previous decade and has a shawl round her shoulders. The three daughters wear more fashionable dresses with fitted bodices and slight bustles. The young woman on the right has a tennis racket and an apron over her dress, but seems to feel the want of a partner.

72 The Yercaud District Social Club meeting, 1907

The style of the building gives away what the clothes do not — that the picture was taken in India. No sartorial concessions have been made to the climate; rather, the subjects show a wholly characteristic determination to pretend that they are still in England.

73 A pair of hockey players, c. 1905

For these two the opportunity to mix with young men was perhaps as great a draw as the game itself. Both girls wear gored skirts of dark cloth, ending above the ankles, and loose matching coats with shoulder capes. They have high-necked blouses and gloves. The girl on the left has a loosely knotted scarf and a tam o' shanter under which her hair is rolled back off her face. She appears to be wearing stout boots. Her friend has a flat, wide-brimmed hat. One contemporary of these two girls lost her team a goal because in putting up her hand to adjust her hat she caught her glove on one of the hatpins and could not disentangle it.

74 Cycling party at Wolfeton House, Dorset, c. 1898

The women wear fashionably-cut cloth costumes with leg-of-mutton sleeves and gored skirts which just clear the ground, gloves, and either boaters or felt hats. Several of them have neckties. The only concession to comfort is in the unbuttoned coats. The men are mostly dressed in Norfolk jackets and knickerbockers, with woollen stockings or puttees and soft, peaked caps.

Helena Swanwick, an enthusiastic cyclist, recalled that,

my long skirt was a nuisance and even a danger. It is an unpleasant experience to be hurled on to stone setts [paving bricks] and find that one's skirt has been so tightly wound round the pedal that one cannot even get up enough to unwind it.

A few daring women adopted knickerbockers for this reason, but the majority struggled on in skirts.

75 A cyclist, c. 1878

The safety bicycle was not invented until 1884. Flora Thompson describes how, in the Lark Rise of the 1880s,

cycling was looked upon as a passing craze and the cyclists in their tight navy knickerbocker suits and pillbox caps with the badge of their club in front were regarded as figures of fun.

This cyclist has completed the outfit with ribbed stockings and stout lace-up shoes.

76 The Dorchester Ramblers Cycling Club, 1900

This is a slightly humbler social group shown on their Easter Monday trip to Lulworth, but their clothes are very similar to those in the preceding picture. The women have high-necked blouses under their mostly double-breasted cloth costumes; the men are all in soft caps. The man second from the right has a rather showy necktie, and the fifth from the left clearly takes rather a pride in his moustache.

77 A pair of cyclists, 1900–5

The girls are identically dressed in floor-length dark skirts, extremely showy blouses with very full sleeves gathered into tight cuffs, black ribbon bows at the neck and wide-brimmed flat hats – ostensibly rather unsuitable get-ups for cycling in. One suspects that the photograph was intended as much to commemorate the outfits as the bicycles. The older couple, who clearly prefer tried and tested means of transport, are conventionally dressed: she in a costume, blouse and hat; he in a dark suit and bowler hat.

78 Motorcyclists, 1910

The riders of this motorcycle with its magnificent basket-work sidecar seem rather formally dressed for the exercise. He wears a three-piece suit and light hat; she has added furs to her costume and blouse and wears a large hat, the crown smothered in flowers.

79 A day at the races, 1909–10

A group of fashionable people calculate their bets in the shelter of their motor car. There is a picnic basket on the grass beside them. The lady on the left is wearing an elaborate costume with a magnificent feathered hat and a satin-lined boa. Her companion also has a fashionably large hat, but wears a simple coat and skirt. The garment hanging over the back of the car is perhaps a duster coat.

80 A touring party at Tregony, 1901

Here the motorists are all wearing loose coats over their ordinary clothes. The figure in the middle has a trilby; the others have soft caps. The locals have come out in force as much to get into the photograph as to admire the De Dion. The little girl on the extreme left and the woman next to the driver clearly cannot believe their eyes, while the old boy on the right thinks the whole thing is a huge joke.

81 A couple in a motor car, c. 1905

The proud motorists are posed outside their house.
He wears a loose-fitting coat with a deep collar, a
soft cap with a peak and gauntlet gloves. She has
a pale jacket with by now rather old-fashioned full
sleeves, gloves, and a flat hat with a veil which
covers her face and ties under her chin. They have
a protective cover over their knees. This photograph
was taken from a postcard; the message on the back
reads:

The veil unfortunately hides Muriel's face,
would not recognise her, would you?

82 The hazards of motoring dress, 1905

A cartoon from Punch *which makes the same point as the postcard writer of the previous picture.*
Expectation: The Browns welcoming the Robinsons (awfully jolly people, don't you know, from whom they have had a letter saying that they will arrive early in the day by motor).
Realisation: The Browns, when the arrivals have removed their motor glasses, etc., disclosing *NOT* the Robinsons but those awful bores, the Smiths.

EXPECTATION.

REALISATION.

83 Holmes School infants' class, c. 1900–10

It is clear that the children's mothers have worked very hard to turn them out creditably. Nearly all the girls have very clean white pinafores, some frilled, over their everyday school dresses, and the boys have spotless collars, many of them surprisingly lacy. One little girl has a very smart dark sailor dress trimmed with white braid. The children sitting in the front row are unconsciously showing off their re-soled boots. The teacher, for whom being photographed is doubtless less of an event, wears a patterned blouse and a simple skirt.

84 Christchurch Yeovil Sunday School outing, 1889

These are teachers and pupils from a fairly well-to-do congregation. So many of the girls are in white, with black sashes or gloves, that it almost amounts to a uniform. There are a large number of fashionably tall hats to be seen. The minister stands in the back row, just to the left of centre, and two young men lurk self-consciously near the extreme right; otherwise, the gathering is entirely female.

85 A group of Etonians, 1907

The boys are buying buttonholes for the 4th June celebration, which commemorates the birthday of George III. All have top hats, striped trousers and highly polished shoes. The boy in the centre has a short jacket and a broad Eton collar, while the other two wear tail coats and wing collars with bow ties – a sartorial distinction based not on age but on height. The flower girl with her squashy hat and stained coat is another Eliza Dolittle.

86 A girl in a pleated dress, 1893–4

This young girl gravely shows off the fullness of her accordion-pleated skirt, worn with the statutory black stockings and kid shoes. Perhaps she is suffering from the scratchy petticoats complained of by Eleanor Farjeon, or perhaps she is just concentrating on holding her pose.

89 A small boy, c. 1890 – 1900

Sailor suits for children first came into fashion in the 1850s, after Queen Victoria had had Bertie painted in one, and they retained their popularity well into this century. This version is of dark cloth, and has knickerbockers fastening at the knee with four buttons instead of long trousers. The jacket has shiny buttons, a lanyard and a somewhat incongruous collar of white openwork embroidery. The outfit is completed by stout lace-up boots.

90 A mother and son, c. 1900

The boy's sailor suit has a bloused top with deep cuffs and long trousers, a scarf passed under the collar and a lanyard. The neck opening is filled by a white dickey. He wears a broad-brimmed round straw hat and carries a pair of gloves. His mother is wearing a beautiful woollen costume with scalloped flounces, a wide falling collar and a large knot of ribbon at the centre front. Her flat hat is trimmed with an upstanding feather, or 'aigrette'. The mother's look of apprehension, and the son's of resolution, suggest that perhaps he was going away to school for the first time.

91 A young cavalier, c. 1904

Outfits like this one, referred to variously as 'cavalier', 'musketeer' and 'Gainsborough' costumes, were favourite dress for pages at society weddings of this time. One imagines that the young wearers may have been less enthusiastic about them than the onlookers.

**92 and 93 Two small boys in Fauntleroy suits,
c. 1879 and early 1880s**

In Frances Hodgson Burnett's novel, when Cedric and his grandfather meet for the first time, 'what the Earl saw was a graceful childish figure in a black velvet suit, with a lace collar, and with lovelocks waving about the handsome, manly little face.' *The mothers behind both these pictures have succeeded pretty well in reproducing this ideal, though in one case the short sleek hair does not quite belong to the image.*

94 Boating at Molesey Lock, 1896

Judging by the queue for boats, this was a popular pastime. It is clearly a hot day because, although a few of the men are in dark suits and felt hats, most are in light flannel trousers, rolled-up shirt sleeves and boaters. Some of the women are in light summer dresses and some in blouses and skirts with neckties and boaters. One or two look distinctly overdressed. Several are carrying sunshades, but only one has put hers up.

95 *A fashion plate from* Le Follet, *1857*

Three society ladies are shown in a box at the theatre. They wear light silk dresses with flounced skirts and low necks, trimmed with lace and flowers, and hold bouquets or fans in their tightly gloved hands. A servant hands a pair of opera glasses to one of them; her silk dress follows the same lines as theirs, but it is dark and the neckline is filled in with pleated muslin up to the throat.

It is said that when crinolines became fashionable, at about the time of this picture, theatre boxes had to be enlarged in order to accommodate them.

96 Theatre audience, 1899

This is a matinée at the Haymarket Theatre. Ladies' hats were so large at this time that ultimately theatres started handing out printed requests to remove them. Sonia Keppel, in Edwardian Daughter, *recalled an occasion in 1905 when a lady took off her hat and pinned it to the back of the seat in front of her, thus accidentally impaling the occupant 'like a gigantic butterfly'.*

97 A day on the river at Richmond, 1900

The lady enquiring about hiring a boat is rather formally dressed in a tight-fitting cloth costume over a high-necked blouse, and a flower-trimmed flat straw hat tilted forwards over her upswept back hair. She has a spotted veil over her face and carries a parasol. Gwen Raverat comments, in Period Piece, that ladies' dresses at this time 'were always made too tight, and the bodices wrinkled laterally from the strain'; this is a perfect example. There is also an awkward point at the bottom of the corset where the skirt refuses to lie smoothly.

98 The Bath and West of England Show at Pottington, 1859

This occasion is again something of a social mixture. The men's clothes range from formal morning dress to the very casual get-up of the figure at the extreme right. The artistic-looking figure in the middle wears a light-coloured informal suit with what seems to be an early form of Norfolk jacket. The advancing lady wears a flounced skirt over a crinoline and a striped shawl; the lady on the left is in mourning.

99 A country fair, c. 1910

The reception committee awaits the arrival of the guest of honour. The worried-looking children in the centre clearly have a part to play: one of the little boys has a Union Jack to wave, and the girl with the muffler and slightly raffish feathered hat holds a bunch of wild flowers. The people with white tickets on their hats are presumably the fair committee.

100 Stallholders at a charity bazaar, c. 1912

Bazaars were an important feature of social life, particularly in the country. This appears to be a confectionery stall, with sweets done up in little fancy boxes, and a witty text inscribed on the canopy above. The three younger women wear very simply cut white dresses with large hats, while the older one on the right has rather overdone things.

101 A fête at Chelmsford, June 1904

Edwardian skirts, so gracefully sinuous in fashion plates, could look quite ungainly when caught by the wind, as has happened to the figure on the left. There was, in fact, quite an art to managing them. The correct procedure was to: grasp the edges of the placket hole with the fingers, not a whole handful, and lift the skirt up on to one hip, resting the hand on the hip without turning the elbow out.' The lady on the right is a perfect illustration. Note the child on the right being restrained by reins.

102 The opening of the new Swing Bridge at Whitby, 24 July 1908

This photograph by Frank Meadow Sutcliffe shows the official party, headed by Mrs Gervais Beckett carrying a large bouquet, leading the procession across the bridge, watched by an eager crowd. There are spectators at the windows; at the left side of the picture a nursemaid holds up a baby, and one adventurous group, including a photographer, has climbed on to a flat roof to get a better view.

103 Prize-giving at a Temperance Fête, 7 July 1910

Temperance societies were formed throughout the nineteenth century, their very numbers suggesting a certain lack of success, though the activities they organized were often well supported. Exactly what is going on in this picture is not clear: the figure at top left carries a besom, and at the other side some children are waving hay-rakes. The figure in the centre wears the traditional countryman's outfit of embroidered linen smock, buttoned breeches and a billycock hat.

104 Presentation to Mrs Col. Bingham, May 1866

This ceremony took place in Dorchester. Earlier in the year Mrs Bingham, whose husband commanded the Dorset militia, had instituted a reading room for the men in the Corn Exchange, where they could be served with tea and coffee. Her venture was highly successful, and to show their gratitude the men collected nearly £10 and bought the rosewood and silver dressing case which she is being presented with in the picture. It was, reported the Dorset County Chronicle, *'a spectacle which filled them with honest pride and pleasure'. The ladies wear light silk dresses over crinolines, mantles of varying lengths, and either broad-stringed bonnets or the increasingly popular hats. Two fringed parasols can be seen at the extreme right of the picture. The men are of course in uniform, though there are two figures in the centre in top hats and frock coats.*

105 A family group in the garden, c. 1864

The marquee and the elaborate floral arrangements suggest that this has been the scene of some sort of garden party. The man wears a frock coat and pale trousers and has put his hat down at his feet. The ladies sit on the ground surrounded by their crinoline skirts; the older one wears a cap while the younger one has removed her narrow-brimmed hat.

106 The Frogpool Choir outing, July 1908

The choir sit in a horse-drawn char-a-banc. The woman following behind wearing a sporty tweed cap is riding side-saddle. The stout figure beside her seems to be wearing a somewhat oversized boater.

107 Bridport Rifle Club, 1908

The figure on the right wears a three-piece suit and a shirt with a pinned collar. The winners of the team shoot look a degree less smart, especially the man in the centre whose jacket is almost scruffy, and who wears an informal knitted cardigan over his striped shirt.

108 Queen Victoria's Golden Jubilee, Wareham, 1887

The crowd is waiting for a procession to come past. They carry banners, one with a portrait of the Queen, one somewhat inappropriately inscribed 'Fear God Honour the King'. At the left of the picture is a large group of small boys in some kind of uniform; a good many of the men present are wearing sola topis. The young girls wear fashionably short skirts.

109 The funeral of Queen Victoria, 1901

Slow came the music and the march, till, in silence, the long line wound in through the park gate... . There it was—the bier of the Queen, coffin of the Age slow passing! And as it went by there came a murmuring groan from all the long line of those who watched, a sound such as Soames had never heard, so unconscious, primitive, deep and wild, that neither he nor any knew whether they had joined in uttering it. Strange sound, indeed! Tribute of an Age to its own death... . Ah! Ah!...The hold on life had slipped. That which had seemed eternal was gone! The Queen— God bless her!

John Galsworthy, In Chancery

110 The proclamation of George V in Yeovil, May 1910

The most striking thing about this picture is the hats. In a comparable crowd today almost everyone would be bareheaded; here only a handful are. Even the babies wear white bonnets.

Suggested Further Reading

Byrde, P., *A Visual History of Costume: The Twentieth Century*, Batsford, 1986.

Davidoff, L., *The Best Circles – Society, Etiquette and the Season*, Croom Helm, 1973.

De Mare, E., *London 1851: The Year of the Great Exhibition*, Folio Society, 1972.

Foster, V., *A Visual History of Costume: The Nineteenth Century*, Batsford, 1984.

Hartnell, N., *Royal Courts of Fashion*, Cassell, 1971.

Manchester City Art Galleries, *Children's Costume*, 1959.

Manchester City Art Galleries, *Costume for Sport*, 1963.

Manchester City Art Galleries, *Weddings*, 1977.

Margetson, S., *Leisure and Pleasure in the Nineteenth Century*, Cassell, 1969.

Taylor, L., *Mourning Dress*, George Allen & Unwin, 1983.

Walkley, C., *The Way to Wear 'em: 150 Years of Punch on Fashion*, Peter Owen, 1986.

Walkley, C., *Welcome Sweet Babe: A Book of Christenings*, Peter Owen, 1987.

Wood, C., *Victorian Panorama*, Faber & Faber, 1976.